After Midnight, Reflections and Thoughts on Life, Love, and Loss.

T.R. Villarreal

All rights reserved. No part of this publication may be reproduced, stored

in a retrieval system, or transmitted in any form by any means, electronic,

mechanical, photocopy, or otherwise, without first obtaining written

permission of the author.

Text copyright © 2014

All rights reserved.

Life

Puzzle Pieces

Someone once said to me
that a life was like a puzzle
made up of many and varied pieces.

It was up to you
to fit those pieces and make a life.

There are pieces of regret
and love, guilt, achievement
and triumph.
pieces of sadness and loss.
pieces of pure joy.

Each in their way make
the picture of your life
and each belongs in its own place.
And together they make
a picture of the man
and this, a life well lived.

Ω

Remembering

Remembering summer smiles
looking back at me,
soft spring dresses flowing,
brown toned legs,
with looks that could kill,
exciting possibilities.

Just ramblings
of a man
looking back
over days long
since passed.

For an old man,
it's the past
that still moves
the heart
at times.

Sometimes, it's those
tender pleasing memories
that lets one live
with longing to make
many, many more.

Ω

I Take This Time

I take this time
to say this silent prayer
and although silent
I say it fervently
with all the strength I have.

Lord bring grace
to those I have loved and
love still.

Let them learn of love
and all that love brings
and what it is to be
of this world and the blessings
that life gives.

Render us compassionate
and forgiving
let us not see differences
only that light
that glows within us all.

Let courage fill our hearts
to love and be loved,
and to feel the life giving
warmth of another.

Ω

I Sit Content

I sit content in my
folding chair in the sun,
while a Western Swallow
patrols his hard fought ground
that is my yard.

I don't mind at all
his territorial prerogative.
He has, after all,
his own mystical
biological imperative.

My presence,
my existence,
is of no consequence
to him. He has
better things to do.

I am perfectly content
to see this gorgeous
butterfly make his circles
in the sky.

His mission is laid out
and perfectly planned.
And I am pleased
in a small and large way
to merely be a witness.

Ω

I Can Close My Eyes

I can close my eyes
and see
the brightest of smiles.

It is a smile
that can light up
the blackest of nights
and banish the darkest of moods.

Imagine if you can
how just a smile
can do all that.

I don't have to imagine
I see it almost
every day and still
it is not enough.

It's a blessing
and a gift
and all I need
to know and show me
that life has meaning,
when I see
that brightest of smiles.

Ω

One Can Feel It

One can feel it deep in the heart
a sense of longing or of
something missing
in this life.
Still, I go about my day
with the hope it won't
tear me apart.

I keep asking, keep wondering
what could it be?
Is it a loss of confidence
or, the sense of time passing
without me?

Maybe it's the need to love
and be loved?
To share and be accepted
as I am?
To give to one who will
appreciate the giving
and be pleased to have
what is offered.

It's an empty void
needing to be filled.
I will keep at giving and giving
until someone accepts
what I give not
as a taking but more
like mutual sharing
of two lives blended
into one.

And let time flow
as it pleases
without me worrying
or have that sense
of loss.

Ω

I Know

When I feel alone
I know, in my heart
I am not.

You are there
to guide me,
to lead me,
to give me direction.

When I feel lost,
I know I am not.
You are there
to whisper,
"come this way".

You lead me
to the light.
Where I am
bathed in the glow
of you.

In your light,
I am warmed,
I am nourished,
and nothing else
is quite as important
as knowing
you are there for me.

All I have to do
is ask
and you come
and you listen
and what I thought, is,
is not.
and what is not,
comes to be.

And it is you,
who makes
it so.
And I know it.

Ω

I LAY ME DOWN

I LAY ME DOWN
ON A BED OF LEAVES
SMELL THE GREEN
OF THE LIVING EARTH
BENEATH ME.

IT'S GOD'S GOOD MATTRESS
THAT SOOTHES THE ACHES
AND PAINS OF LIVING.

I SEE THE STARS ABOVE
MOVING ON THEIR UNKNOWN PATH.
I CAN FEEL THE EARTH BREATHING
AND I WONDER
WHAT WORDS CAN DESCRIBE
THIS SENSE OF BEING.

FOR A SHORT SPAN
I AM WITHOUT FEAR
AND I GATHER STRENGTH
TO CONTINUE MY OWN PATH
AND WONDER WHERE
THIS PATH I CHOOSE
WILL LEAD ME.

Ω

THIS DIRT

There is a certain deliverance
in this dirt I work.
It delivers me
absolution from the asphalt.

It surrounds me in comfort
and beauty.
And for most, that should
be enough.

To me, it delivers much more.
It brings me back
to my beginnings,
when my mother would
hand me beans to plant.

I would take each and
prepare a special place
for it to grow.
for the first new leaves to show.

After days, each little plant
would curl and reach for the sun
like a child reaching for its
mother's arms.

Years from that time,
I still do my planting
and wait and wonder
at each new leaf.

Absolution arrives
and forgiveness,
and countless mysteries
explained.

And in working that dirt
I am refreshed,
and blessed beyond
my most fervent prayers.

Ω

A LIFE WELL LIVED

A life well lived
is much more
then the sum of its parts,
it is memories made
and kindnesses received
and gladly given.

It is of lessons learned
by example
and by doing
and tender mercies
conveyed with a smile
or gentle touch.

And all is remembered
and cherished
knowing,
all was given from the heart.

This life is the ultimate expression
of family
that distance can not diminish
nor time extinguish.

It is the meaning
and the essence
of what it is
to love and be loved.

This life, is your life
and to me
and all others who
love you,
and have been loved by you,
it makes all the difference.

Ω

A FATHER'S PRAYER

Consider this child,
who before my eyes
has grown to be a man.

I ask one thing
and that is for you
to hold him tight
in your arms
when I am no longer
there to do so.

Allow him to grow straight,
with kindness
and compassion
to know right from wrong
to take the time
to consider the beauty
and the blessings
that surround him.

Grant this father's wish,
banish all worry,
all anxiety and allow
the best part of my heart
to continue beating in his.

I ask that you align
all your angels
like an army
around him
so that the miracle
and the meaning
of his birth
can be fulfilled.

This is my one and
only prayer:
Consider with tender kindness
my beautiful precious child.

Ω

LOVE

In the final analysis,
after all is said and done,
after a life well lived,
I have come to know
there is one
true thing;
the love you give,
gives back to you.

If we believe in the
sacred man,
if we believe in
Christian/Judeo principles
there has to be love.

Love is there.
Love will get you through.
Yes, love will conquer hate
and make you a better
for it.

When life is tough
and anxious and
unkind, learn to love
and give love.

Love is the greatest gift
and its a gift
with a better return
then any life investment
you will ever make.

Love comes in many forms
and many means.

Where there is poverty
give what you can.
When there is a need
be there to give of yourself.
Where there is sorrow
provide compassion.

Where there is loss,
give comfort.
Where there is sadness,
be there if only
to listen.
Where there is anger
replace it with
an understanding love.

Never leave someone
to suffer alone.

In this fleeting moment
called life,
learn this one key lesson:
Give love and more love.
And your path to the light
will be assured
and you
and this world
will be the better for it.

Ω

THIS TREE

I am covered by the canopy
of my own pine tree.
It stands tall and proud.
It has grandeur and has grace,
and spreads its limbs out wide
like a welcoming embrace.

The branches so thick, even
the rain does not penetrate.
I smell only the sweet perfume
of the morning shower.

This tree is mighty and magnificently
majestic and its mine,
my part of the American dream.
I may own it, if that can truly be said
but its beauty
is for the benefit of the many.

it provides my neighbors
and me with oxygen,
the birds a place to live,
the squirrels a place to frolic,
and eat and the occasional
raccoon a place to scamper
and reach the highest bough
thinking it is safe from me.

Of course, it is safe.
This tree welcomes all visits and visitors.
This tree is a place of sanctuary
and of solace.
And offers only the best of itself
to others and to me.

Ω

A NIGHT OF MIDNIGHT SHOWERS

It was a night to cherish
a time to hold dear
just laying out on a blanket
in the dark of night
looking to the heavens
to see the grace of God
streak across the sky.

I had everything I needed
as he lay next to me
to share this time.
A time for me to expound on
the wonders of nature and
the natural world.

If he was impressed
I don't know, and
really, was not my aim.
All I knew, all I cared about,
was this time with my son.

Those streaks across the sky
like stings of magical pearls
flung across the midnight sky
leaving trails, thrilled me
beyond measure.

I was content and in
perfect bliss and I was
surrounded by all
that mattered in life.

That night, God granted
me proof of her existence
and gave me the gift
of a sublime and pleasing
time with my beautiful boy.

Ω

DESTINY

What is the destiny of men?
Is it to conquer the world,
or merely be a part of it,
or somewhere in between?

I must confess, I still
seek mine.
Someone admired, once said to me,
"turn to the light
and it will shine the way".

And so, with each passing day
I turn toward the light
and that day turns to two
and two turns to many
and still I go forward.
seeking.

My hope still intact.
With each mistake made,
and there have been many,
I learn.

At times, my grasp
exceeds my limit.
Yet the effort is made
no time for empty gestures.

In a life well lived,
where lessons have been learned,
I make each day remembered
each word kind
or at least spoken without malice.

And still, I seek that true light.
With each day, I see it more and more clear.
I keep to the well lit path.
And when the time comes
as it does to us all
when I am bathed in its warmth,

it is with the audacity of hope
that my destiny may be answered
somewhere,
among those many days
of living with my compass
bearing toward the light

Ω

You Can See Them

You can see them
along the long central valley
browner then the dirt
they work
hands gnarled
and rough hewn
bodies bent to the soil

they are the ones
who pick the crops
you can choose
at your leisure along
the air conditioned aisles
of your superstore

they choose to break
the law to take
those jobs that
no one wants or
no one chooses to do

these are the people
who end up bent and broken
not so much to pick your crops
rather to provide bread
and a life for their families

and someday when justice
prevails their sons and daughters
will prevail themselves
and pass that sense of sacrifice
of their elders to their own

and in that path
of selfless sacrifice
and back breaking work
we will learn there
is value and meaning
to the labor that they do

Ω

WHO KNOWS

Who knows what dwells
in the hearts of men?
When the weight of the world
is just too much to bear.
Or when the noise of the world
drowns out the better nature
in us all.

We give in,
time and time again.
Never hoping for the worst
and yet too tempted to say no.
In the end, its fatigue
that makes cowards
of us all.

And so we leave others
to suffer the consequences
of the sorrow and the loss.

Ω

Love

ONE LOOK

One look is all
that's needed
I see what you offer
as you guide me
to paradise
I see you before me
the glistening glow
of you
the warmth
the wetness
the slippery
openness
I hear your
song
of pleasure
leading to ecstasy
I get lost in you
while I whiff
the secret scent
of you
it is there
all I need
all I will ever need
all that I would
ever want.

Ω

THE AIR I BREATHE

I sometimes wonder if
the air I breathe
is the same as
the air she breathes.
It is strange this
distant connection
with a common thread
that binds us.
Even far away she feels
close and never distant
one look, one luscious curve,
is all I need to bridge
this wide gulf to allow
me close to her
to let everything else
disappear into meaningless
nothing
and I am left with only
this fresh air we breathe
together.

Ω

IN MY DREAMS

In my dreams
she is bathed in sunshine,
smooth and glowing skin.

I can see the
natural light is
in love with her.
It was made,
especially for her.

See her stand
in the sunlight
sparkling.
See her move
so serene,
her body like
a dream.

You can tell
she is in her element,
shiny hair,
glimmering golden
against the blue
of the sky.

Radiant and pleasing
smile, she offers it
to anyone who
is lucky enough
to receive it.

To me, that smile
is the best and most
fortunate gift of all.
And, I readily accept it
and am pleased,
every single day.

My sunshine arrives
by way of that
radiant, wonderful smile.

Ω

IN HER ARMS

I can turn to her and say
"baby baby"
and she is in my arms
to warm and comfort me
to sooth any sorrows
or lift my spirits
or just to say hello
in that special way
of hers.

With her, it doesn't take much
just her arms around me
with an embrace
that says so much
and does much more
and takes me to a place
we both know.

It's all I need
all I could ever want
and all that this life
is meant to be
when one allows
another to come in
and simply share
for the sake of sharing.

With me,
it's enough to know
and a constant comfort
to be welcome in her arms.

Ω

I TURN TO YOU

When the fates are unkind
I turn to you.

When distance divides
I turn to you.

When hope is diminished
I turn to you.

There is no circumstance,
there is no instance,
when, I can not turn to you.

Every fear is conquered.
Every unkind word forgotten.
Every burden lifted, when
I turn to you.

And in all the treasure
of this world,
in every magic potion
ever made,
there is none
that would equal you.

You have in your possession
an unequalled power.
Handed to you freely,
delivered to your door willingly,
placed at your feet humbly,
by me.

Let it be known
that in that treasure trove
of power possessed
within your being,
I derive all the benefits
much too numerous
to name, when
I turn to you.

Ω

BLUE MOON

Did you notice the blue moon
on New Year's Eve?
It just reflected my blue mood
knowing you are
at a distance.

Far away from my arms
and embraces.
Far away from my kisses
and my hands to reach you.

I am surprised its not
always blue.
Because every day
I want you.

My arms should be
allowed to take you in,
to hold you close
to feel the warmth of you.

Once, within my reach,
you would never escape.
And I would be free
to feel your heat
and smell your wonderful
and powerful perfume
that only your body makes.

It would be a paradise.
I could not escape,
nor would I want to.

Ω

I REMEMBER

I remember she would sleep
in a short silk spaghetti strap
slip, those straps constantly off
her shoulders.

She looked like Elizabeth Taylor
in Cat on a Hot Tin Roof only
if you can imagine,
much more gorgeous.

Her glowing golden legs
showing enough to drive
me wild. That soft silken
slip showing her beautiful
breasts from the side.

You would probably recognize
her in a Leonard Cohen song
without any of the sad pretensions.
Seeing her was a reward
and the recognition that there
is a God.

I recall to the last detail
her coming in the spring
and the summer of her going.
Years that should
be best left forgotten,
but never will.

Ω

AS I TURN TOWARD HER

As I turn toward her
I feel the warmth of her
even before the first touch

The light from the window
illuminates curves of thighs
and hips

And the smell of her hair
and her skin sustain me
only she is capable
of supplying suspicions of life
within me
that were never there before.

Ω

A DAY CAN PASS

Without you,
a day can pass
and I still stand
but never more than two.
It's a matter of survival.
For I am addicted.
It is like a craving
that must be assuaged.

I need that smile, that glow
that turn of hand and look.
It soothes and comforts me.
It gives me all I want
to survive beyond mere
existence.

So if you want to know
don't leave me alone
beyond a day without you.
It is all I can do.
It's all I can take.
It's beyond my capacity
to make it past a day,
without you.

Ω

HOW DOES ONE EXPRESS

How does one express
what love is to another?
What does one say
to convey the meaning
of such an emotion?

What the heart feels
the brain can't always
say in mere words.

It is much more
then I love you's
much more then
an expression of words.

It is a combination
of joy mixed with
apprehension mixed
with the pain
of rejection.

And yet we say it
time and time again
because to not say it
brings it own terrible
combination of emotions.

I love you,
I adore you,
I worship you.
Pick your sweet, sweet poison
Only you know when
the time is right or not.

The saying: Better to have loved
and lost, then to never loved at all,
needs refinement.
It carries it own fifty shades
of grey.

It can only kill you
or make your life fulfilled.
And sometimes the two
are indistinguishable from
the other.

And yet, we must
say it and we do.
Time and time again.

Ω

SECRET SILENT SONG

It's a secret silent song
I sing to you.
One that only you can hear
if you listen close and
put your mouth to mine.

You will hear soft and easy
moans that build and build
as we discover each other
with that liquid noise of passion.

Quiet words that lead
and guide us to the ultimate
sound of all
hearing us overcome with
that special rush that sends
shock waves through us both.

Where we are left with
fruitless efforts and attempts
to catch our breath
and let our pounding hearts
come back to normal.

Without saying any further
words
you will hear
that I still want you
and the only sounds
we hear
are the sounds that touching
makes on your gorgeous
skin with my mouth and lips
and fingers.

That secret silent song
that no one hears but you
will continue throughout
the night and
will vibrate and reverberate
from my body to yours.

Ω

LESSONS

She would say "you have taught me so much
and I have learned to be myself".
And I just listen and know the truth.
All that was taught, all the lessons learned,
began and end with you.

What she presumed to be lessons,
to be teachings,
were nothing more than the realization
that it was all in her from the start.

She was allowed to be who she is
to be what she felt
to show all that she wished to
without the need to hide
or be concerned.

Does a star in the sky wonder
of its beauty from afar?
Does the most striking flower
contemplate its own splendor?

Neither has the need.
It is what it is,
Some things are as they are
ravishing and glorious,
a wonder to behold.

It is for those of us
fortunate enough to behold
such wondrous things
who need to kneel
and give our thanks
to the God or Gods
who made it possible
for us to behold and
to exist in their presence.

Ω

WHEN THE DAY ENDS

When the day ends
and the night
reclaims the quiet,
I turn to thoughts of you.

That alone can put me
in another world,
where things go well,
where stress and tension
are banished, where
even ordinary things,
take on a more lustrous
hue.

It can be just a look
or just a thought
and I drift away
and be in another place
where a certain peace
comes to claim me
and I realize
what it means to be alive.

It's the power
of your image.
The power that you possess
over me.
And to tell you
the truth,
I don't mind at all
that you know.

Ω

CUANDO EL DIA TERMINA

Cuando el día termina
y la noche reclama la tranquilidad
doy vuelta a los pensamientos
de tu.

Ese solo puede ponerme
en otro mundo,
donde van las cosas bien,
donde la tensión se desaparece,
donde cosas ordinarias,
toman una tonalidad
más brillante.

Puede ser apenas una mirada
o apenas un pensamiento
y mi encuentro lejos
y estoy en otro lugar
donde cierta paz viene
a reclamarme y conosco
qué significa ser vivo.

Es la poder
de tu imagen.
La poder que tu tienes
sobre mí.
Y te digo la verdad
no mi importa que
lo sabes.

Ω

WE ARE WHERE WE ARE

I can close my eyes
and see you just as you are
in any time in your life.
And it is so because you
share your life with me
and allow me to see you,
natural and beautiful.

We are where we are
because you desire it so
and accept and
have no need to
put up obstacles
or boundaries.

We have no need
for answers
to questions
of how we
came to be.

What the head
sometimes asks,
the heart, cannot
always answer.

At this place,
at this time,
it is enough to know
that we are.

Ω

I WILL STAY

When the night
brings on the quiet
and you feel alone
let me be there
just to hold you close
and keep the demons
at bay.

I will stay
until the day
breaks
and all that is left
is you
and my arms
around you
until you say
let go.

I will
dry your eyes
and see you through
the night
and listen to your sighs
and comfort you
and keep you
until the morning light.

Ω

LOSS

WITHOUT YOU

Without you,
it only takes a day or two
and the world is not the same,
the sun is not as bright,
the night becomes even darker
and life itself somehow changes,
without you.

People pass in ones and twos
sometimes more.
They pass without a clue.
But I know something is different
that something has gone awry
and I am the lesser for it
and its all because I am
without you.

The essence of a life worth living
is somehow missing
the chemistry has changed
I am left without and broken
when I find myself
without you.

Ω

LOST LOVE

If there can be anything
good to be said
about a lost love
it may be this;

that once lost
the remembrance
of her smooth skin,
the light of her
gorgeous eyes,

the form and curves
of her,
her voice
delicate and lyrical,
the feel and the touch
of her will always
stay the same.

Years may pass,
time will take
its toll
but the beauty,
the warmth and
tenderness of her,
will remain as always.

Burned and buried
deep within.
Those remembered,
tender, torturous
unmerciful memories
of you.

Ω

JUST ONE LOOK

All it took was just one look
and it was never quite the same.
Colors became brighter,
every step, I walked seemed lighter.
Even the air I breathed felt
perfumed and full of life.

She was a dream of the Gods.
For only Gods can make perfection.
Yet for me, she was real
even if from a distance.

The Gods made her with powers
that is vested only in a few.
Endowed with what every man wants
but, doesn't know until she appears.

She could make time and distance
disappear. As she did for me.
She could make grown men tremble,
with the fear of never seeing her again.

In form and shape, she was perfection.
In temperament, as well.
Crying babies stopped their weeping
when she came near.

Women wished they were her,
and men wished they were with her.
And I took it all in with appreciation
and anticipation every time.

She had an intimate independence
preferring to be herself.
Needing no man or woman
to tell her who she is.

When she walked it was
with a weightless gait
knowing every step she took
led her in a path of her own choosing.

Never needing a map or directions,
not compass or GPS.
She charted her own course,
and kept it.
To an unheard rhythm of her own.

And I followed every step.
Content to know she consented
with my decision to spend some time
with her from afar.

And in my world, that made all the
difference.

And sometimes, just sometimes,
if I stopped to clearly listen,
I swear, I could hear
her sweet and soothing voice
whisper just what I wanted
to hear.

Ω

SI ESTOY MURIENDO

Si estoy muriendo
después de unos o muchos años
le pido a Dios
para algunas más respiraciones
apenas para besar tus labios calientes suaves
para mantenerte cerca
para permitir el calor de tu cuerpo
a pasar con el mío

Sacrificaría alegre
ésas respiraciones ultimas
conocer al señor
amado me bastante
para permitirme
a estar en tus brazos
una ultima vez
y conteste a mi ultimo rezo.

IF I AM DYING

If I am dying
of a life of
a few or many years,
I would ask the Lord
for a few more breaths,
just to kiss your soft
warm lips
to hold you close
to allow the warmth
of your tender heart
to pass through mine.

I would gladly
sacrifice any remaining
breaths,
knowing the Lord
loved me enough
to allow me
to be in your arms
one more time
and answer my last prayer.

Ω

I CAN REMEMBER

I can remember her hair
tumbling down around her shoulders
gold like wheat
sparkling in the sun

and when she smiled
her golden eyes reflected
the smallest light like
flecks of gold

she could light
the darkest room
by just walking in
and every head
would turn toward her
with a silent acknowledgement
of her radiance and beauty

and she would say hello
in her casual way
without ever knowing
how truly beautiful she was
but I was glad
and always pleased
to enjoy that lovely way
of hers

For me, the best part
was seeing in her eyes
how she looked at me
and knowing that special look
was just for me and only me.

Years later, I remember
her still
and always will.
Not with sadness
just joy and jubilation
at knowing every part
of who she was.

Ω

AFTER SHE LEFT

After she left
the days drifted
and passed as
in slow motion,

the nights, even
slower.
Now I am left
only with memories.

And yet, I know
it must be so.
It's the penance
that must be paid.

It's the cost of
assuming, I was the one.

In the end,
one assumes,
one believes,
one dreams,
at the peril
of the unknown
demons
at the door.

Ω

A SIMPLE WISH

When I am done and gone
burn my bones until dust
and heave my ashes upon
this good green earth
and pray that my soul
will journey through elysian fields
until I am home.

Let that my dust
feed this good and giving globe
that gave me nothing but joy
and comfort.
My blessings were many,
my rewards were immense.

I take comfort
that this meager dust
may feed the soil
so that seeds
will prosper and grow
perhaps sempervirens
ever green and ever strong.

God grant that my bones
and ashes nourish
and allow to flourish
something left behind
long after I am
done and gone.

Ω

A DOOR CLOSES

A door closes
and its dark
for a long, long while
and it feels
like no light
can penetrate this mood
and sorrow
I am left with.

And people say
it gets better with time
but time is made of
seconds and minutes
and hours that can
cut to the bone.

The dark will not leave me
but that's alright
I can endure.
Knowing that it's a loss
I can survive because
it is a price
worth paying
for loving you
and for your unintentional
leaving.

I know
the time will come
when we meet again
and your warm embrace
and the sound of your laughter
will make it right
once more.

It is that hope,
no that promise,
that allows me
to endure.
And I shall,
for you and for me.

Ω

SHE WAS A WOMAN

She was a woman
who would make any man
want to follow
just to see her body
sway to an unheard tune.
Not that she was a temptress
that was not part of
her makeup although
she could play the part
if she chose
and play it very well.

Her approach was more direct
her beauty captured you
and put you off to anyone
or anything else until she
she allowed you in.

I was fortunate to spend
two summers and a fall
following her and loving
every minute until
her magical and mystical
spell was broken
and I fell back to earth,
believing in aliens
from then on.

Ω

WHEN GOD WANTS TO PUNISH ME

When God wants to punish me
he brings you back to me
in my dreams
and for that time
I am lost in you.

It is then that I understand
what it means to love and
what it means to live
as if nothing else on earth
matters.

It is then that I can touch you
and let my fingers tremble
smoothly sliding softly on your skin.

Breathing the smell of you
watching your every move,
impossibly intoxicated and drunk,
there is no explaining
your affect on me.

Morning comes too soon
and I am left destitute and desolate
praying
for the night to come again
and again
with no regard for the day.

Ω

WHEREVER YOU ARE

Wherever you are,
I am there with you.
When you look at the
evening sky,
I see the same canopy of
stars.

However far removed
we are from one another,
our closeness removes
the miles.

The intimacy that exists
between us
allows me to forget.
It allows me to know
we breathe the same air,
we see the same stars
and moon

It allows me
to take in your perfume,
to sense the feel and touch
of you, to become a part
of nothing else, but you.

I can taste you
because I have tasted
you before.
I can dream of you
because you invade my dreams.

I can go wild and
be myself with you
because you say
yes to me.

It is as if we were
separated at birth
and now, by some twist of fate,
we find ourselves
living in separate places.

Now destiny has dared
to bring
us back together.
Even as the miles continue
to exist between us.

We are of the same vibrations
the same persuasions
there is an intimate and invisible
thread that binds us close.

It is that closeness,
the intimacy we share,
the same thoughts,
the same wants and desires,
that continues to connect us.

What we have is more
then most will ever have
and more than most,
would even dare
to hope for.

Ω

WHO KNOWS THIS SONG

Who knows this song I sing?
More importantly, who hears it?
Who is there to know what I say
and hears my heart when I do?

No one now.
No one to listen,
to commiserate.
And I am resigned to that fate
it is terrible but tolerable.

Given the circumstances,
I will take what the fates allow
and keep the faith at least
in my heart and in my hopes.

I will not dwell on what is
I will dwell in what was
and the lovely memories
and the incredible sense of her
as I sleep.

I won't fear the nights
and I will hurry the days
to end, so I can feel her again.

It is then that I know
my song is heard
and understood and
I am forgiven and absolved
and loved for me.

It is then that the terrible
becomes tolerable.
I will accept that for now
and thank the Gods gladly,
for allowing me to have her
for the time I did.

And I will thank them
even more when they
guide me back to her.

Ω

WHERE IS SHE NOW

Where is she now
and how is she?
Does she pine like me?
Does she remember
how it was
and how it might have been?

All I know is how
it is with me
and how it is still.

I live in memories made
and memories of my
own making.
Not able to distinguish
between the two.

In time I have learned
It is enough
to know
that I knew her when
and knew her at her best
and how I wish
it could still be so.

Ω

THE YEARS FLY BY

FOR JASON

The years fly by like minutes
but the memories remain.
A child is born, and
for the first time
you understand what love is
and you realize
how it is possible
to feel how
your heart beats
outside your own body.

And you nurture
and guide and have
great expectations,
when really, truly,
all you wish
is for happiness
to dwell in their hearts.

Soon, in rapid sucession,
the years pass.
One follows another
until the child
becomes the man
with children of his own
and the heart that was his
and yours, continues,
to beat in them

It is the eternal cycle
of men and women,
of birth and death and renewal.
And the lesson to learn;
to always keep
close to your heart,
is to cherish what is given
and what sometimes,
too soon, is taken away.

Ω

WHISPERS

She whispered in my ear,
like a gentle wind blowing.
"Stay, stay with me".

I sensed but did not hear,
heard but did not sense
the urgency in her sounds.

I left, to seek my dreams.
Not knowing how strong
I would feel her tug.

Never imagining how
I would miss her,
how I would be unable
to dream
without her.

Now, I am still away.
Left with only cruel,
sweet memories,
and bereft of dreams.

She is there still.
whispering to another,
who hears and senses
every sound and cherishes
every whisper.

Ω

11/12/18

TO: GRADY

Hope you enjoy
All The Best
[signature]

Made in the USA
San Bernardino, CA
06 November 2014